INVISIBLE WORLDS

Earth's Secrets

James Bow

mc **Marshall Cavendish**
Benchmark

New York

Other Marshall Cavendish Offices:
Marshall Cavendish International (Asia) Private Limited, 1 New Industrial Road, Singapore 536196 • Marshall Cavendish International (Thailand)
Co Ltd. 253 Asoke, 12th Flr, Sukhumvit 21 Road, Klongtoey Nua, Wattana, Bangkok 10110, Thailand • Marshall Cavendish (Malaysia) Sdn Bhd,
Times Subang, Lot 46, Subang Hi-Tech Industrial Park, Batu Tiga, 40000 Shah Alam, Selangor Darul Ehsan, Malaysia

Marshall Cavendish is a trademark of Times Publishing Limited

All websites were available and accurate when this book was sent to press.

Library of Congress Cataloging-in-Publication Data
Bow, James.
Earth's Secrets / by James Bow.
p. cm. — (Invisible worlds)
"Describes the invisible forces responsible for shaping life on Earth"—Provided by publisher.
Includes bibliographical references and index.
ISBN 978-0-7614-4196-0
1. Geodynamics—Juvenile literature. 2. Earth sciences—Remote sensing—Juvenile literature.
3. Earth—Remote sensing—Juvenile literature. 4. Climatology—Remote sensing—Juvenile literature. I. Title.
QE501.25.B69 2011
550—dc22   2009052362

Series created by The Brown Reference Group
www.brownreference.com

For The Brown Reference Group:
Editor: Leon Gray
Designer: Joan Curtis
Picture Managers: Sophie Mortimer and Clare Newman
Picture Researcher: Sean Hannaway
Illustrator: MW Digital Graphics
Managing Editor: Miranda Smith
Design Manager: David Poole
Editorial Director: Lindsey Lowe
Children's Publisher: Anne O'Daly

Consultant: Dr. Donald R Franceschetti

Front cover: Science Photo Library/Andrew Syred; inset: Shutterstock

The photographs in this book are used by permission and through the courtesy of:
Corbis: 14, Stephen Frink 21, Dennis Kunkel Microscopy, Inc/Visuals Unlimited 26, NASA/JPL–Caltech 9, Ken Redding 33, Roger Ressmeyer 39,
George Steinmetz 10–11, 28 (bottom), 36; NASA: Apollo Gallery 7, Earth Observatory 13, 18, 34, GSF 4–5, APOD 44, Landsat 42, NOAA 16,
Visible Earth 15, 19, 22, 32; NOAA: 24; PA Photos: AP 17; Satellite Imaging Corporation: 35; Science Photo Library: Ed Adams/Montana State
University i, 29; Eye of Science: 27 (top), NASA 8, 23, 28 (top), 31, Daniel Sambraus 41, Chris Satleberger 37, U.S. Geological Survey 25;
Shutterstock: Videowokart 27 (bottom); Wikipedia Commons 40.

Printed in Malaysia (T)
1 3 5 6 4 2

Contents

Earth's Secrets

Invisible forces affect our lives every day. Hidden currents of air drive Earth's weather systems. Currents moving around the world's oceans determine how cool or warm the weather will be. Forces deep within Earth's crust cause volcanoes to erupt and violent earthquakes to shake the ground. These same forces create valuable resources, such as precious metals and petroleum. They also give farmers fertile soil in which to grow their crops.

Scientists are learning more about the hidden forces that are shaping our world. Every day, images from satellites in orbit around Earth help **meteorologists** predict the weather. Oceanographers also use sound waves to map the seafloor. Advances in science and technology are helping to unravel many of Earth's mysteries.

This view of Earth is a combination of different images taken by cameras on a satellite. Satellites help us look at things we cannot see from the surface of our planet.

CHAPTER 1

Earth from Space

People did not understand what Earth looked like as a whole until they looked at it from above. Aerial photography became a reality when hot-air balloons and airplanes took to the skies. Aerial photographs showed the planet as it had never been seen before.

The first satellite image of Earth was taken by *Explorer 6* on August 14, 1959. As more satellite images followed, violent **hurricanes**, hidden rivers, and even the remains of lost civilizations were seen from space. Satellite images also helped make sense of the world and its place in the Solar System.

Scientists use other clues to make their observations. For example, a satellite image cannot measure the temperature of the atmosphere. So scientists measure the amount of chemicals in the atmosphere. This gives them an idea of how warm or cool the air is. It is like identifying an animal by studying its footprints.

Scientists cannot always see what they are looking for using their eyes alone. Visible light is just one form of **radiation**. Other forms of radiation can make normally invisible things "visible." For example, **infrared** can detect rain in the clouds.

The "Blue Marble" is one of the most famous satellite images of Earth. It was taken by the crew of *Apollo 17* in 1972.

Remote Sensing

Remote sensing is looking at people and objects that are too far away to touch. Most people use their eyes to see things. During the Civil War, from 1861 to 1865, soldiers used telescopes in hot-air balloons to identify enemy positions. During World War I, from 1914 to 1918, pilots carried cameras in their airplanes to take pictures of the enemy. Modern technology helps people to see much farther. For example, spy satellites take pictures of enemy positions from space.

Different waves

The light that we can see is made up of waves of energy, called radiation. Each color we see is made up of waves of the same length—from the longest (red) to the shortest (violet). There are different types of radiation. Infrared radiation has longer waves than those of red light.

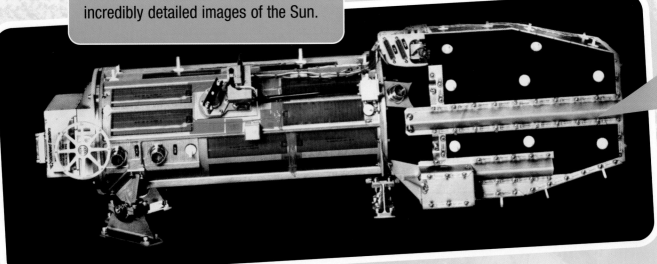

NASA's Extreme ultraviolet imaging telescope enables scientists to take incredibly detailed images of the Sun.

Radio waves and microwaves are even longer. Ultraviolet light has shorter waves than violet light. **X rays** and **gamma rays** are even shorter. All the different waves of energy, from radio waves to gamma rays, can be used to look at things that our eyes cannot see—or that might be too dangerous to get near. One common example is the X rays that doctors use to look inside the body for broken bones.

? Did You Know?

Radar is remote sensing using radio waves. During World War II, the British used radar to detect enemy planes. To keep it a secret, the British said their pilots had good vision because they ate a lot of carrots. The myth that carrots are good for vision was born!

Close Up

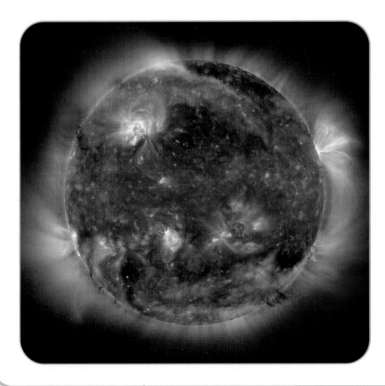

The Extreme ultraviolet imaging telescope takes pictures of the Sun using ultraviolet light. Unlike visible light, ultraviolet light can reveal the solar corona in incredible detail (left). The telescope then beams the images back to Earth. The solar corona is the hot "atmosphere" of plasma that surrounds the Sun and extends for millions of miles into space.

Satellites and Remote Sensing

Remote sensing can be passive or active. Passive remote sensing measures the natural energy that is produced by, or reflected off, an object. A good example is aerial photography—light reflects off Earth's surface and is captured on film by a camera. Active remote sensing involves hitting an object with a beam of energy and studying the reflections. Radar is an example of active remote sensing.

Reflection detection

Remote sensing relies on sensitive instruments to detect the reflected radiation. Different instruments capture these signals across a wide range of wavelengths.

Remote sensing instruments are vital tools for scientists. Some are so sensitive that they can detect the radiation of chemicals that make up stars in distant galaxies.

Landsat

Scientists have learned so much about our own planet thanks to remote sensing from satellites. Since 1972, the Landsat program has provided millions of satellite images of Earth. Jointly run by the National Aeronautics and Space Administration (NASA) and the U.S. Geological Survey, Landsat has been important in many different

Air traffic controllers use radar to identify the altitude, direction, and speed of airplanes at a busy airport.

areas of research, from agriculture, conservation, and mapmaking to surveillance and national security.

Landsat images of Earth can reveal objects that measure between 50 and 200 feet (15 and 60 meters) in size. The first Landsat satellite, *Landsat 1,* was launched on July 23, 1972. Since then, six more Landsat satellites have been launched. Two of them (*Landsat 5* and *Landsat 7*) are still in operation. The next stage in the program is the Landsat Data Continuity Mission (LDCM), which will continue to capture detailed images of Earth from space. NASA is due to launch the next Landsat satellite in this mission in 2012.

Close Up

The word *radar* stands for Radio Detection and Ranging. German scientist Christian Hülsmeyer came up with the invention in 1904, but it took another thirty years to become practical to use. A radar system has a transmitter that beams radio waves at a target. A receiver picks up the reflected radiation and amplifies the signal, making it stronger. Both the transmitter and receiver are usually located in the same place. Using radar, police officers can check the speed of cars and meteorologists can detect changes inside a thunderstorm.

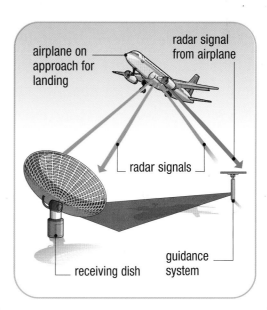

airplane on approach for landing

radar signal from airplane

radar signals

receiving dish

guidance system

CHAPTER 2

Weather and Climate

Predicting the weather is more than just figuring out if it will be sunny one day or raining the next. The weather changes day by day, but year by year it forms a distinct pattern. Predicting the weather also involves figuring out whether the winter will be mild or harsh or if the seasonal rains will come at all. People plan their lives around the weather. In Bangladesh and India, farmers depend on the monsoon rains to water their paddy fields. The Inuit of Greenland and North America depend on freezing cold winters to keep the ice on which they live and hunt.

Predicting the weather is very difficult because there is so much weather to look at. Earth's weather systems are all interconnected. So a change in the patterns of weather can lead to devastating droughts in one country and widespread flooding in another.

The changing pattern of weather over a long period is called **climate**. Scientists are only just learning how the climate of the world works and produces the weather we see from day to day. Human activities are affecting the climate, so we can only guess what the weather will be like in the future.

Satellite images reveal things we cannot see from Earth. This satellite image shows Hurricane Katrina as it hit the Gulf Coast of the United States on August 29, 2005.

Global Weather

These white clouds are traveling along in the jet stream. This current of air forms a boundary between cold air over the north polar region and warm air over the tropics.

Earth's weather systems are driven by the Sun. As heat strikes Earth's surface, it warms the air and the oceans. Less direct sunlight hits the poles than the Equator. As a result, cold air sits over the polar regions, and warm air sits over tropical regions near the Equator.

Hot air rises over the tropical regions, and cold air sinks over the polar regions. This produces a cycle of wind between the poles and the Equator. Earth also rotates as it spins around the Sun. This produces swirling masses of air around the planet. The current of air flowing between these swirling air masses is called the **jet stream**.

The Sun also heats up the land and the sea differently. It heats up land quickly, but the land releases heat to the air just as quickly. The water in the oceans takes longer to warm up but releases heat to the air more slowly. This creates more changes to the air above.

Ocean currents

As water gets colder and saltier, it sinks to the bottom of the sea. This

Climate factors

Other elements that affect climate include **altitude** and **humidity**. The air cannot hold heat or moisture very well at high altitude. As a result, it is much cooler and drier. At low altitude, the air is more humid, holds heat for longer, and makes rain more likely.

Different factors contribute to climate change. Natural changes include a shift in the position of the continents or even how hot the Sun burns. But human activities such as deforestation and burning **fossil fuels** are also speeding up the process of climate change.

movement of water produces currents of warm and cold water in the world's oceans. The **Gulf stream** is an ocean current that brings warm water from the Caribbean across the Atlantic Ocean to European waters. The Gulf stream is part of the Global Conveyor Belt—a network of cold and warm currents circulating through all the oceans.

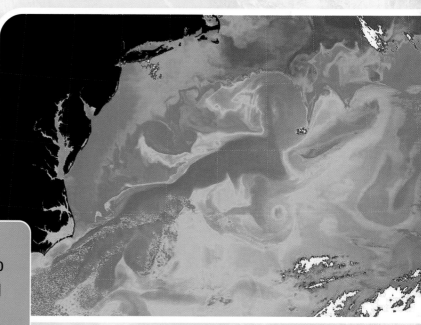

The Gulf stream brings warm water (shown in red) from the Caribbean to Europe. The East Coast of the United States is shown in black.

Predicting the Weather

Before satellites existed, weather forecasters used visible clues to predict the weather. The ancient Babylonians were the first weather forecasters. From 650 BCE, they started to recognize patterns of clouds in the skies. Early weather prediction was often based on folklore. One saying goes: "Mares tails and mackerel scales, tall ships carry short sails." This may seem strange, but there was sense in it. Sailors, whose lives depend on accurate weather forecasting, noticed that clouds—today known as altocumulus and cirrus clouds—resembled the scales of fish and the tails of horses. Whenever they saw these clouds, bad weather usually followed in the next 36 hours.

This satellite image shows the "Storm of the Century" building up over the Eastern seaboard of the United States in 1993.

Measuring the weather

The invention of machines such as the barometer allowed forecasters to measure the weather using invisible clues. Barometers measure air pressure. Low air pressure is a good indication that stormy weather is on the way. In 1835, the invention of the telegraph helped forecasters

Close Up

In 1993, the "Storm of the Century" struck the east coast of the United States. Birmingham, Alabama, received 17 inches (43.2 centimeters) of snow. Four feet (1.25 m) fell in Chattanooga, Tennessee. Cities that far south could not handle the snow and had to shut down. Temperatures dropped to record lows in 26 states, and there were 11 confirmed tornadoes. The storm killed 300 and caused $10 billion in damage.

to relay their reports to forecasters in other places to tell them what weather was on its way.

As the technology became better, weather forecasters gained a better understanding of how the weather worked. In 1922, British scientist Lewis Fry Richardson (1881–1953) suggested that math could be used to predict the weather. His theory became a reality when computerized forecasting started in the 1950s. At the same time, the first satellites were launched and gave forecasters even more data to study.

? Did You Know?

There is some truth in the saying "Red sky at night, sailor's delight. Red sky in the morning, sailor's warning." A red sunset means that the Sun is shining through dust in the air. High pressure is moving in from the west, and good weather is likely. A red sunrise reflects the dust of a system that is moving away, and bad weather is likely.

Weather Satellites

A satellite image reveals thick cloud cover over the Great Lakes in North America.

Weather satellites help forecasters study things they cannot "see" from the ground. Geostationary weather satellites orbit at 22, 375 miles (35,800 kilometers) above Earth's surface. These satellites appear to be fixed over the same point on Earth, as if they are attached by a piece of string. Even so, geostationary satellites can observe a wide area of the planet. The National Oceanic and Atmospheric Administration (NOAA) has two satellites that monitor the weather of North America, but there are 16 more satellites in operation. Some are polar-orbiting satellites, which orbit the planet from the North Pole to the South Pole around 530 miles (850 km) above the surface. These satellites are "Sun-synchronous," because they orbit over the same area at the same local time. Polar-orbiting satellites gather more

? Did You Know?

Vanguard 2 was the first weather satellite. NASA launched it in 1959 to study cloud cover. The satellite took pictures for the first 300 days after its launch but then crashed.

Modern meteorology

Satellites provide clear images of weather systems—at a distance. Weather forecasters still need close-up observations to figure out what is really going on. It is hard to judge the wind speed of a hurricane from a satellite, so hurricane hunters fly airplanes into storms to gather the data. Direct observation may be the easiest to study the weather, but all of the tools are used together to make meteorology a more precise science than it was just decades ago.

detailed images than geostationary satellites because they orbit closer to the surface of the planet.

Satellite imagery

Normal cameras on satellites capture visible images of clouds in daylight. Weather forecasters use these images to identify weather fronts and storms. Thermal or infrared images are used to determine what type of clouds make up the weather system, how high they are, as well as surface temperatures on land and at sea.

Weather satellites can be used to track the progress of forest fires such as this one in Viejas, east of San Diego in California.

CHAPTER 3

The Blue Planet

Water hides things and can be hidden itself. We know little about what goes on beneath the water's surface. Yet it is only with water that life can exist.

If all the water on Earth could be stored in a cube, each side of the cube would be 700 miles (1,115 km) long—about the same distance as between Chicago and Washington, D.C. All this water covers around 70 percent of Earth's surface, but only 3 percent of it is freshwater.

When a lot of water moves, there is almost no holding it back. When Hurricane Katrina first hit land in southern Florida in August 2005, the U.S. National Hurricane Center gave it the lowest Category 1 rating. As it swept over the warm waters of the Gulf of Mexico, the hurricane grew into a Category 5 monster. When it hit land for the second time in New Orleans a few days later, winds of up 120 miles (200 km) per hour swept the city. A storm surge 25 feet (8 m) high broke the levees that protected New Orleans and submerged the city. The flooding swept far inland across the Gulf Coast of Alabama and Louisiana. The hurricane was bad enough, but it was the storm surge that did most of the damage over the wider area.

A school of minnows seek shelter in an underwater cavern. The world's oceans hide an amazing variety of living things, and we are only starting to learn more about them.

Tracking a Watery World

Sea currents are rivers of water in the ocean. The currents swirl warm water toward the polar regions and cold water back to the Equator. The gravitational pull of the Moon and the Sun also move the oceans. Sea levels rise and fall across the world. These are called tides. In the Bay of Fundy in Canada, the sea is shallow and enveloped by land. The tides there can rise and fall by as much as 56 feet (17 m) during the day.

Studying the seas

NOAA measures ocean currents using drifters. As their name suggests, these devices "drift" on the water's surface and transmit data

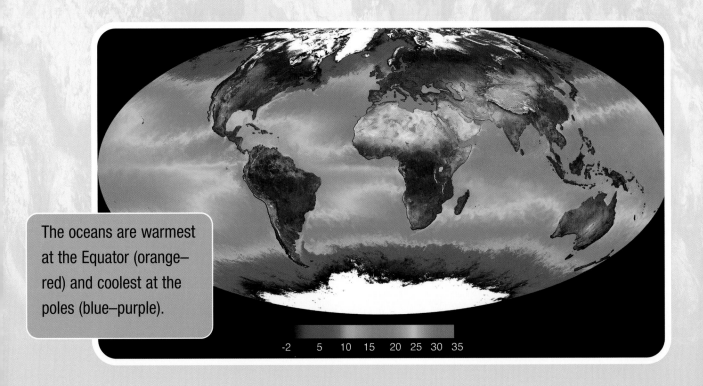

The oceans are warmest at the Equator (orange–red) and coolest at the poles (blue–purple).

-2   5   10   15   20   25   30   35

? Did You Know?

Most waves are the result of the wind. The wind speed, the amount of ocean the wind gets to blow on (called the fetch), the length of time the wind gets to blow, and the depth of the water all contribute to the size of the waves.

information such as sea surface temperature and wave height and send the data back to shore. A modern development is wave radar, which uses radio waves or **lasers** to measure changes in the surface of the ocean remotely, without risking life or limb.

such as sea temperature and position back to scientists on land. Drifters have revealed a lot about the movement of Earth's complex ocean currents.

Satellites help NOAA chart the progress of storms and record the temperature of the ocean water. Satellites can even chart the color of the ocean, which is a measure of the color of plants in the water, plumes of sediment from rivers, and oil spills.

Other information is gathered by buoys floating in the middle of the ocean. These buoys record

A NOAA satellite image picks up an oil spill off the coast of Lebanon in 2006.

Underwater Topography

The bottom of the ocean is an extreme environment. About one mile (1.6 km) below the surface of the Pacific Ocean, vents called "black smokers" shoot up mineral-rich water into the ocean depths.

Fast Facts

- At 35,788 feet (10,911 m) below sea level, the Mariana Trench is the deepest point on Earth.

- At 55,000 miles (88,000 km) long, the Mid-Ocean Ridge is the world's largest mountain chain.

A black smoker shoots mineral-rich water into the ocean, providing support for many different sea creatures.

These hydrothermal vents are the centers of large ecosystems where most life could not usually exist. The organisms that live there do not take energy from the Sun because it is so far down. Instead, they get their warmth from **magma** on the ocean floor. The magma heats up the water to 750°F (400°C), but the water does not boil because pressure at the bottom of the ocean is too great.

The crew of a small **submersible** called Alvin discovered these vents in 1977. Before then, the technology did not exist to explore the seafloor. The enormous underwater pressure involved made diving impossible. Scientists thought that the ocean floor was so extreme that nothing could live there.

Seeing in sound

Scientists cannot see the ocean floor directly, but they can use sound to create a picture for them. The idea of "seeing in sound" was born when

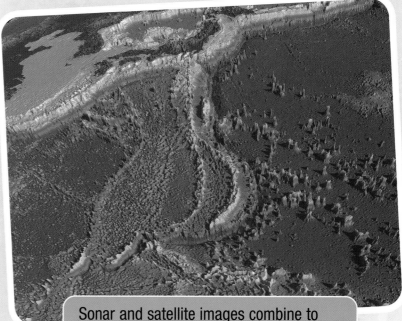

Sonar and satellite images combine to show the deepest point on Earth—the Mariana Trench (purple) on the Pacific Ocean floor.

? Did You Know?

Sound travels faster in water than in air. It also travels faster in saltwater than freshwater and at different speeds depending on the water temperature. Measuring the differences in the speed of sound can help detect currents.

the first submersibles were built at the start of the twentieth century. The use of submarines during World War I and World War II led to the development of **sonar** (Sound Navigation and Ranging) to protect vessels from attack. Submariners also needed accurate maps of the seafloor, called bathometric maps, to guide them through the ocean depths. Modern bathometric maps are incredibly detailed. They have revealed mountain ranges and deep trenches at the bottom of the sea.

Life in the Water

Microscopic plankton called radiolaria come in a variety of beautiful shapes.

Life on Earth cannot survive without water. Look at a drop of seawater under a microscope and you might see it is full of **plankton**. These tiny creatures are food for many other sea creatures. Without plankton, other sea creatures higher in the **food chain** would starve.

? Did You Know?

Occasionally, red tides engulf the coastline around Florida. Red tides are caused by too much of an algae called *Karenia brevis* in the water. Sometimes the algae produce a toxin that kills fish. The toxin is not deadly to people, but it can still cause respiratory and skin problems.

Studying ocean life

Scientists have come up with many new inventions to study hard-to-see ocean life. Scientists travel to the ocean depths in submersibles, which can withstand the huge pressure in deep water, to study ocean life up close. Sometimes plantlike plankton called algae grow out of control and form vast "blooms" in the water. Scientists use satellites to track the growth of these blooms.

Close Up

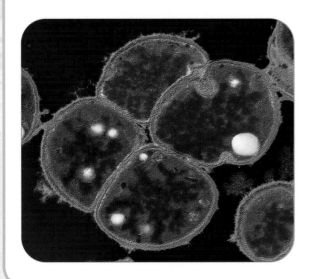

Life can exist almost anywhere on Earth where there is water. Similar to the black smokers on the ocean floor, the hot springs of Yellowstone National Park bring hot, mineral-rich waters to the surface. Microorganisms called extremophiles (left) thrive in the hot, acidic waters that would kill most other creatures. These **bacteria** give the springs their brilliant colors.

Sediment Profile Imagery

The extreme conditions make it difficult to study anything at the bottom of the ocean. Trying to look under the muddy seabed is even harder. Scientists use Sediment Profile Imagery (SPI) to look into the silty layer of the ocean floor to study the chemical processes at work. A wedge-shaped detector is dropped into the ocean and pierces the silt on the seabed. The detector collects data and transmits the results back to the surface. SPI is similar to the way space probes look for signs of life on other planets.

Microscopic creatures turn the hot springs of Yellowstone National Park a brilliant golden-brown color.

Glaciers

About 68 percent of the world's freshwater is hidden inside glaciers. Glaciers feed rivers that would normally run dry. Scientists can look at glaciers to learn about past climates.

Glacier formation

Glaciers form when snow builds up in one place for a year or more. In glacier formation, new snow is called névé while snow that stays around for a year or more is called firn. As the firn builds up, its weight presses down on the snow below, turning it into ice. Years of compaction presses the air out of the ice, turning the glacier blue. Eventually, the glacier starts to move under its own weight to form a slow-moving river of ice.

This Landsat image of the Bering Glacier in Alaska shows that the ice has retreated. Scientists think that global warming is to blame.

In the past

Ten thousand years ago, glaciers covered North America and

Scientists measure an ice core sample drilled from a glacier in Greenland to find out how the climate has changed over tens of thousands of years.

Europe. In the 1830s, scientists figured out that there was an ice age by looking at the land formations the retreating glaciers left behind, such as marks on rocks and valleys.

Retreat of the glaciers

Glaciers are melting because our planet is getting hotter. If all the ice in the world's glaciers melted, sea levels would rise by 230 feet (70 m). Cities around the world would flood. Glaciers are melting very quickly in some parts of the world. For example, the glaciers of the Rocky Mountains in Alberta, Canada, have melted and retreated more than half a mile (1 km) in the last 125 years. In Africa, the slopes of Mount Kilimanjaro in Kenya, have lost 80 percent of their ice cover. Some scientists worry that all of the ice on Mount Kilimanjaro could be gone completely by 2040.

Close Up

Glaciers offer a glimpse back in time. Ice core samples drilled out of the glaciers of Greenland contain ice that was frozen 100,000 years ago and never thawed. Scientists are studying the tiny bubbles of air, particles of dirt (left), and the remains of microscopic bacteria and plant life that are trapped in the ice. They hope to learn more about the conditions on Earth 100,000 years ago.

CHAPTER 4

Lay of the Land

The ground on which we stand might seem stable, but every so often the planet reminds people of the violent forces that are taking place beneath its surface.

Early in the morning of April 29, 1903, a large chunk of limestone broke off the eastern face of Turtle Mountain in western Alberta, Canada. The limestone tumbled down the cliff and into the valley below. The mining town of Frank lay directly in its path. Of the 600 people who lived in the town, 100 were in the path of the falling chunks of limestone. More than 70 people were killed, but only twelve bodies were recovered from the rubble. The scar the landslide left is visible to this day.

The land is constantly changing, but it is happening so slowly that we cannot see it. These invisible forces are taking down mountains and cutting deep valleys toward the sea. People are also changing the landscape by farming more land and building new cities.

Following disasters such as the Turtle Mountain landslide, scientists started to look for clues that might prevent similar tragedies from happening. They looked for changes in the land that might offer some warning about when a disaster might occur.

This Landsat image of Turtle Mountain in Alberta shows the pink cliff faces exposed by the landslide that destroyed Frank in 1903.

Mapping the Land

This image of the Grand Canyon was taken by NASA's Terra satellite. The deep canyon has been carved over millions of years by the Colorado River.

Many countries have mapped their land features in great detail. They have produced detailed maps to show where places are in relation to each other and how high they are above sea level. They need to know this information to fix borders or to find the best route for a new road through a mountain pass.

Surveying techniques

Global Positioning Systems (GPS) are devices that pinpoint an object's location on Earth. They work using

? Did You Know?

The world's highest mountain is named for British surveyor George Everest (1790–1866). He measured Mount Everest's height correctly as 29,000 feet (8,841 m). Everest then recorded the measurement as 29,002 feet—so people would not think that it was an estimate.

Close Up

Surveyors map the land using a theodolite. The surveyor starts at a known distance (x) from the point to be measured—in this case the height of the mountain (h). The surveyor sights the summit through the theodolite. The theodolite measures the angle (a) between the line x and the height of the mountain. The surveyor then uses x, h, and a to calculate the height of the mountain.

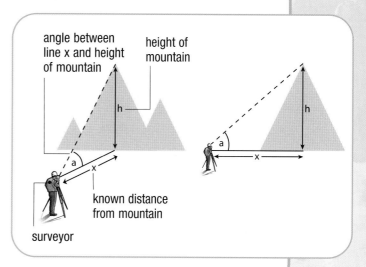

angle between line x and height of mountain

height of mountain

h

a

x

known distance from mountain

surveyor

a

x

h

signals from different satellites. The GPS device measures the angle between each satellite and compares it to known points on Earth. Using all this information, the GPS device calculates the location of the person.

Despite the advances in satellite technology, many surveyors still map the land using measurements taken from Earth. All the maps produced by Britain's national mapping agency, the Ordnance Survey, use **geometry** to figure out the height of points on the map. This is known as the direct surveying method.

A surveyor uses a theodolite to measure the height of a mountain.

Land Use

Scientists do not take detailed measurements of the land. For example, a survey of the rain forest would not try to measure every tree. Instead, scientists pick a selection of trees at random to get an idea of what the population might look like as a whole. So if five trees out of ten are fig trees, then scientists can say with some confidence that half the forest is made up of fig trees. If the scientists pick more trees, they can be sure that the sample is more representative of the population as a whole. This is remote sensing with mathematics. Computers help log and gather the information and

Hundreds of satellite photos have been combined into one image that shows the lights of cities across the United States. Satellites take pictures that scientists cannot see from Earth's surface.

This image shows the Dzibilchaltun pre-Columbian archaeological site in the Yucatán Peninsula of Mexico. It was captured by the GeoEye-1 satellite.

even help researchers link the data from different surveys.

Eye in the sky

The remote sensing data scientists use to measure ocean currents and weather patterns can also be used to study how people use the planet. Satellites can map the lights that illuminate the night sky, and they have measured the heat generated by the major cities.

Satellites can even identify lost civilizations. Archaeologists have found Mayan cities and roads by tracking changes in the Mexican forest. Satellite images have also found ancient villages in untouched areas of rain forest in western Brazil.

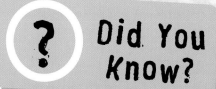

? Did You Know?

Many farmers are turning to remote sensing to grow more crops. Satellite images can reveal changes in the health of crops. Farmers can then use GPS technology to pinpoint where nutrients or water are most needed. This is called precision farming.

Earth's Resources

A line of seismic vibration trucks, or "thumper trucks," pound the frozen land of Prudhoe Bay in Alaska. They send vibrations through the ground in search of oil.

In 1849, American carpenter James Wilson Marshall (1810–1885) struck gold in California. His discovery sparked the 1849 Gold Rush. His discovery was a lucky find close to the surface. This was also the case when American businessman James Miller Williams (1818–1890) dug a well at Black Creek in Ontario, Canada, in August, 1859. Instead of finding water, oil gushed to the surface. His discovery marked the start of the petroleum industry in North America. People rushed to the area to dig more wells. The town of Black Creek changed its name to Oil Springs.

As the demand for petroleum, precious metals, and minerals increased, the existing sources soon dried up. People had to look harder, and develop new technologies, to find alternative sources hidden underneath Earth's surface.

Fossil fuels

Coal and oil are both the fossilized remains of plants and animals that lived millions of years ago. Deposits of these "fossil fuels" are trapped

Close Up

Seismic testing measures the shock waves of an explosion or vibrations created by thumper trucks to generate images of underground rock layers. The shock waves or vibrations bounce off the different rock layers and are picked up by microphones called "geophones." Scientists can then draw a picture of rock layers and find the areas where oil is most likely to collect.

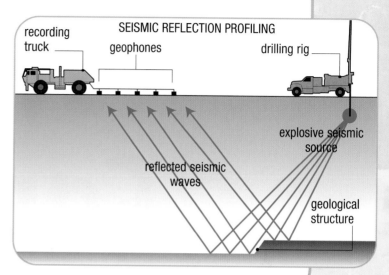

SEISMIC REFLECTION PROFILING

recording truck

geophones

drilling rig

explosive seismic source

reflected seismic waves

geological structure

deep beneath Earth's surface under layers of rock. The earliest **prospectors** had to dig exploratory wells to see the makeup of the rock below. Today, finding trapped oil deposits is much quicker. Modern prospectors use seismic testing to generate images of oil trapped in the rock layers. Prospectors also look for fossil fuels by measuring small changes in Earth's magnetic field. For example, oil deposits are often trapped in nonmagnetic rock. A drop in the magnetic field may indicate a deposit of rocks where oil has collected.

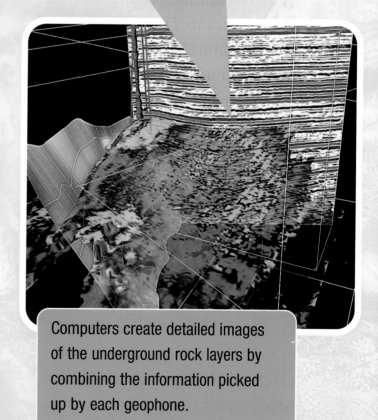

Computers create detailed images of the underground rock layers by combining the information picked up by each geophone.

CHAPTER 5

Moving Earth

In ancient times, people thought that volcanoes were the work of supernatural forces. The ancient Greeks blamed the eruptions on their gods. German astronomer Johannes Kepler (1571–1630) later called them "ducts [channels] for Earth's tears."

One of the most devastating volcanoes occurred in April 1815, when Mount Tambora in Indonesia exploded. The sound of the explosion was heard more than 1,250 miles (2,000 km) away in Sumatra, but the effects of the volcano were felt around the world. Around 11,000 people died following the eruption, which sent large clouds of ash and dust into the atmosphere. The year 1816 became known as the "Year Without a Summer." Crops failed as far away as North America and Europe. Thousands died of hunger.

People only began to understand volcanoes when they realized that Earth is not stable and that the land that makes up the continents is constantly on the move. Forces deep beneath the surface are building up mountains and carving huge ridges under the sea. These forces are still at work today. But how do scientists measure the invisible forces that cause earthquakes and volcanoes and create landforms such as mountains?

A river of **lava** pours from Mount Etna in Sicily, Italy, following an eruption in 1992.

Plates of Rock

In 1596, Belgian mapmaker Abraham Ortelius (1527–1598) noticed that the eastern coast of South America could fit almost perfectly with the western coast of Africa—almost as if the two pieces were part of a global jigsaw puzzle. But if the two continents were once joined, how did they move apart? In 1912, German scientist Alfred Wegener (1880–1930) proposed his theory of continental drift. Wegener suggested that the continents were moving on plates of Earth's crust, floating on a molten "basalt sea."

At first, geologists did not take Wegener's findings very seriously. But the evidence built up, and they eventually came to accept his ideas. Scientists now know that Earth's crust is made up of a layer of cool, rigid rock, called the lithosphere. The lithosphere is broken up into 70 plates that "float" on the asthenosphere, which is a sea of molten rock. As the plates move around, they bump into each other.

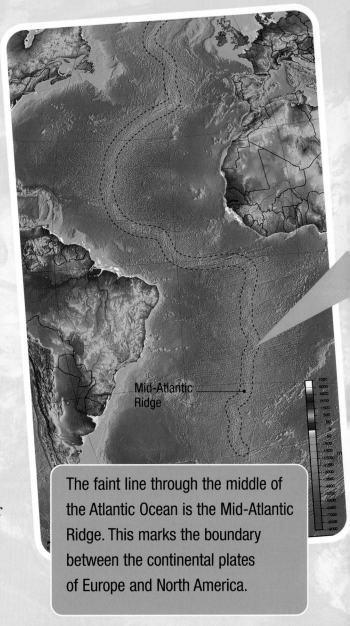

Mid-Atlantic Ridge

The faint line through the middle of the Atlantic Ocean is the Mid-Atlantic Ridge. This marks the boundary between the continental plates of Europe and North America.

Hidden forces

In some areas, the plates are pushing apart. These areas are

Close Up

The Mid-Atlantic Ridge splits two halves of the planet. It marks the point where the continental plates of North and South America push against Africa and Europe. The Mid-Atlantic Ridge forms a huge mountain range under the depths of the Atlantic Ocean, pushing the continental plates apart by up to 1.6 inches (4 cm) per year— about the same rate as your fingernails grow. In Iceland, the Mid-Atlantic Ridge is visible as a large crack in the rocks at Earth's surface. The ridge is almost splitting the country in two.

divergent plate boundaries, such as the Mid-Atlantic Ridge. Plates also meet at convergent boundaries, where one plate slips, or subducts, beneath the other and melts in the asthenosphere. Volcanoes often form in these areas. Where plates slide or grind past each other, they are called transform boundaries. Earthquakes can happen anywhere along a transform boundary. As the plates slide against each other, the grinding forces build up and release in one moment. The San Andreas Fault in California is a transform boundary.

? Did You Know?

Evidence of volcanic activity has been found on other planets in the Solar System. But there are no signs of volcanoes on Venus, which scientists see as the most similar planet to Earth. One theory is that the water on Earth lubricates the plates enough to allow them to move against each other. On Venus, it is too hot for water to exist.

Earthquakes and Volcanoes

On December 24, 2004, an earthquake struck off the coast of Sumatra in Indonesia. It produced a giant wave, called a tsunami, that swept across the Indian Ocean and hit coastlines across Southeast Asia and East Africa. Almost 230,000 people died.

Earthquake detection

Scientists want to predict when the next quake will strike, but it is hard to study forces acting inside

These two photos show before (top) and after (below) the tsunami hit Aceh in Indonesia in 2004. The force of the tsunami killed the green vegetation and reshaped the coastline.

? Did You Know?

The damage from an underwater quake can be felt far from its origin. The wave of water it produces can travel for miles across the ocean before it hits land without warning.

Earth's crust. Often, all they can do is measure the quake as it happens. Scientists use a seismograph to study earthquakes. A seismograph

Close Up

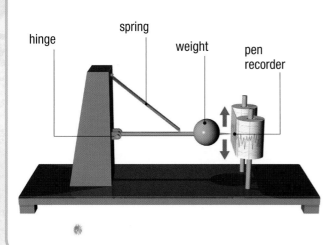

hinge · spring · weight · pen recorder

A modern seismograph is made up of a heavy weight suspended in the middle of the device. The weight can move independently of the machine. When an earthquake shakes the machine, the heavy weight moves slightly later. The movement of the weight is then plotted on a graph. Modern seismographs include electronic sensors and amplifiers to record a wide range of earth vibrations.

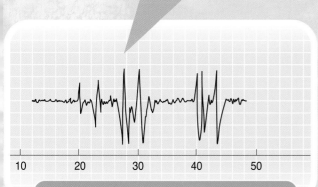

The seismograph plots a chart called a seismogram. This is a record of the underground vibrations (seismic waves) caused by the quake.

predict quakes in advance—by detecting changes in weather conditions and animal behavior—but so far nothing has worked.

Quake watch

Scientists watch for the signs of a quake as it happens. Spotting the main waves can prevent the damage and loss of life caused by the waves that follow. It might only provide a few seconds warning, but it gives people enough time to run to shelter. It might also be possible to shut off gas, water, and electricity, reducing the chance of flooding and fires after the quake hits.

can tell where a quake is occurring, and how big it is, but it cannot say if one is about to happen. Scientists have tried inventing instruments to

Volcanoes

Just like earthquakes, volcanoes are terrifying forces of nature. Some volcanoes do not erupt for decades. People often settle on the volcano's slopes, attracted by the fertile soil. Then one day without warning, the volcano might explode to life, raining down molten rock, called lava, as well as clouds of ash and superheated gases.

Volcano prediction

Volcanoes have caused some of the worst natural disasters of all time. However, there is hope that scientists may soon be able to predict the eruptions. Volcanoes are easier to study because scientists can look at them to spot the warning signs of a potential eruption. Scientists also use thermal monitoring to measure the temperature of the ground beneath the volcano. Rising ground temperatures might indicate that magma is slowly rising to the surface.

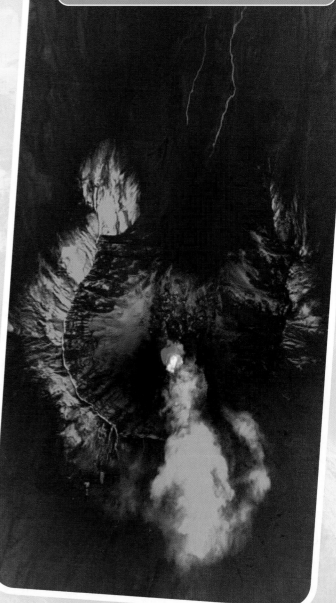

This satellite image captures the eruption of Mount St. Helens in May 1980. Within a few minutes, the blast devastated the area for miles around. Volcanic ash rose more than 15 miles (24 km) into the sky.

Changes in the behavior of nearby geysers, lakes, and rivers can also suggest that an eruption may be building up. Scientists also drill boreholes to measure the level of groundwater. Rising groundwater suggests that gas pressures are building beneath the volcano. A sudden drop in pressure indicates that an eruption may be on the way.

Unfortunately, it is impossible to be completely sure that a volcano is about to erupt. Many volcanoes have looked like they were about to erupt but have remained dormant. If the experts issue too many false alarms, people might then start to ignore future warnings.

? Did You Know?

In 1991, Mount Pinatubo in the Philippines looked like it might erupt. The authorities evacuated 60,000 people who lived near the volcano. On June 15, the volcano erupted, covering much of the country in ash. More than 300 people died—but the evacuation saved thousands of lives.

Conclusion

A dog can hear a whistle at a pitch too high for human hearing. And an elephant can hear sounds at a pitch too low, such as the early shockwaves of an earthquake, and flee to safety early. Scientists know that birds can detect the changes in air pressure due to an approaching storm and fly to safety. Many long-term predictions, such as the ability of the woolly caterpillar to predict a long winter, may be myths. But many animals seem to be in tune with the world around them and react quicker to threats people simply cannot see.

But this does not mean that people cannot understand the hidden forces that shape our planet. Over the centuries, scientists have developed the technology to see beyond what their eyes and ears tell them. This technology will not prevent a natural disaster from occurring. But it has started to help scientists figure out some of the Earth's mysterious secrets.

Glossary

altitude An object's altitude is its height above sea level.

bacteria Bacteria are microscopic living things that reproduce by dividing in two.

climate The climate is the average weather conditions of an area over many years.

food chain A food chain is the feeding relationships between living things in a particular area.

fossil fuels Coal, oil, and natural gas are fossil fuels. They are made from the remains of animals and plants that lived millions of years ago.

gamma rays A gamma ray is a very high-energy form of radiation. Some atoms release gamma rays during radioactive decay.

geometry Geometry is the branch of math that describes the size, position, and shape of objects.

Gulf stream The Gulf stream is a warm ocean current that flows from the Gulf of Mexico north through the Atlantic Ocean.

humidity The amount of water vapor in the air is called humidity.

hurricane A hurricane is a severe tropical storm with rain and winds in excess of 74 miles (120 km) per hour.

infrared A form of radiation called infrared is given out by hot objects, such as the human body.

jet stream The jet stream is a high-speed current of air high in the atmosphere, moving from the west to the east.

laser A laser is a beam of very pure visible light.

lava Lava is molten rock that flows on Earth's surface

magma Magma is molten rock that flows below Earth's surface.

meteorologists Scientists who try to predict the weather are called meteorologists.

plankton Plankton are tiny animals and plants that live in water.

prospector A prospector searches for valuable minerals such as precious metals and fossil fuels.

radar *RA*dio *D*etection *A*nd *R*anging uses radio waves to find objects and calculate their speed.

radiation Energy that moves in the form of waves, rays, or particles is known as radiation.

radio waves A form of radiation called radio waves is used to send TV, radar, and radio signals.

sonar *SO*und *N*avigation *A*nd *R*anging uses sound to find objects and calculate their speed.

submersible An underwater vessel called a submersible is used to explore the depths of the ocean.

X ray An X ray is a form of radiation used to take pictures of the insides of the human body.

Find Out More

Books

Jennings, Terry. *Earthquakes and Tsunamis*. North Mankato, Minnesota: Smart Apple Media, 2009.

Landau, Elaine. *Earth*. Danbury, Connecticut: Children's Press, 2008.

Lindop, Laurie. *Venturing The Deep Sea*. Breckenridge, Colorado: Twenty-First Century Books, 2005.

Noonan, Diana. *People Who Predict*. Huntington Beach, California: Teacher Created Materials, 2008.

Stewart, Melissa. *Earthquakes and Volcanoes FYI*. New York: HarperCollins Publishers, 2008.

Websites

http://landsat.gsfc.nasa.gov/
Visit the National Aeronautics and Space Administration website to find out about the Landsat Data Continuity Mission (LDCM).

http://oceanexplorer.noaa.gov/technology/tools/tools.html
Visit the website of the National Oceanic and Atmospheric Administration to find out about the tools scientists use to study the oceans.

http://science.howstuffworks.com/climate-weather-channel.htm
The How Stuff Works website is a great source of information about climate and weather patterns around the world.

http://www.wovo.org/
The World Organization of Volcano Observatories website monitors active volcanoes around the world, warning people about possible eruptions.

Index

Page numbers in **boldface** are illustrations.